the Indians Knew

By TILLIE S. PINE

Pictures by EZRA JACK KEATS

Adapted for Lucky Book Club

SCHOLASTIC BOOK SERVICES
NEW YORK · TORONTO · LONDON · AUCKLAND · SYDNEY · TOKYO

*Other books by Tillie S. Pine and Joseph Levine
published by Whittlesey House, McGraw-Hill:*

*MAGNETS AND HOW TO USE THEM

THE PILGRIMS KNEW

THE CHINESE KNEW

THE ESKIMOS KNEW

**Also available in a paperbound edition
from Scholastic Book Services*

7th printing .... December 1972
Printed in the U.S.A.

This book is dedicated to
Stanley Weiss and Joseph Levine
for their invaluable assistance

The Indians who lived in our country
long, long ago knew how to do many things
that we do today.

They knew

—how to send messages from hill to hill

—how to make plants grow better

—how to keep food from spoiling

—how to start a fire without matches

—how to drill holes

—how to make paints and dyes

—how to use the moon as a calendar.

The Indians had many good ideas.
They knew how to do many things
that helped them in their day-to-day living.

This book shows you how to try out
some of these ideas.

The Indians knew

that wood can be bent to make things go flying
through the air.

They bent wood into bows.

They used the bows to make arrows go flying
through the air.

Today

divers use a wooden diving board.

The weight of the diver bends the board.

When he jumps, the board straightens.

This pushes the diver up. It makes him go

flying through the air.

You

can prove that wood can be bent

to make things move fast.

Hold one end of a wooden ruler on the table.

Hold it so that most of the ruler sticks out

over the edge.

Put an eraser on the free end of the ruler.

Then bend the free end down and quickly let it go.

The eraser will fly into the air.

The Indians knew

that smoke and warm air go up.

The Indians liked to have a fire
in the tepee. They would sit around
the fire. And they would listen
to the wise man tell stories.
But they did not want the tepee full of smoke.
So they left an opening at the top of the tepee.
The smoke would go up and out through the hole.

The Indians knew how to send smoke messages
to their friends.

They built a campfire. The smoke
from the campfire went high up into the air.
They covered and uncovered the fire quickly
with a blanket. This made puffs of smoke.

When their friends saw the smoke puffs,
they understood the message.

Today

we build tall chimneys in fireplaces.
The chimneys let the smoke go up and out.

When a room is too warm, we open windows
at the top. The warm air goes up and out.
The best way to make a room cool is
to open windows at the top.

You

can prove that warm air and smoke go up.
Blow up a balloon. Now hold it over
a warm radiator. The radiator will warm the air
in the balloon. The warm air will make
the balloon go up.

Hold a strip of thin paper over a warm radiator.
See how the warm air over the radiator
lifts the paper.

Watch when someone blows out a match.
See how the smoke goes up.

9

The Indians knew

how to make hollow boats
to carry things on the water.

Some Indians knew
how to shape buffalo hides
into boats.
Some Indians shaped the bark
of trees into canoes.

These boats were light and hollow.
They could float on the water.

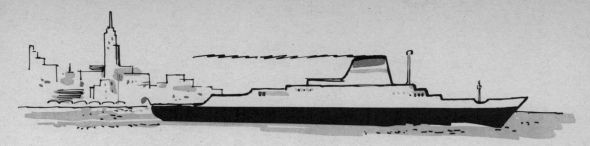

Today

we make small rowboats and large ships.
We shape them so that they can travel on water.
Large ships have many hollow spaces inside
to keep them afloat.

You

can prove how the shape of a thing helps
it to carry other things on water.

Put some water in a pan. Put a piece of paper
on the water. Now put some pennies on the paper.
The paper will sink.

Now fold a piece of paper into the shape of a box.
Put the paper box with some pennies in it
on the water. The box-shaped paper
will carry the coins. It will not sink
until the water soaks the paper.

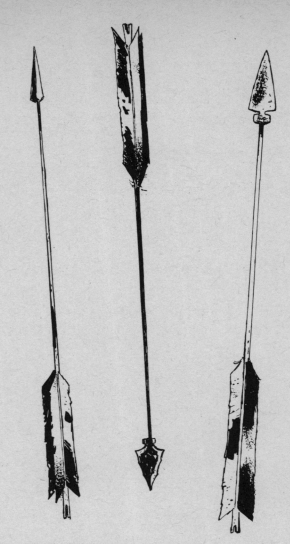

The Indians knew

how to make an arrow fly straight
through the air.

They put feathers at the end of the arrow.
This made the arrow fly in a straight line.

Today

we build "tail fins" on airplanes to help
the planes fly in a straight line.

You

can find out how to make a drinking straw
fly through the air in a straight line.
Throw a straw across the room.
The straw will fall to the ground at once.

You can make this straw fly through the air.
First, make two cuts in one end of the straw, like this:

Now cut out two little pieces of paper.
These will be the "tail fins."

Make a cut up the middle of each tail fin.

Now put one of the tails fins into the straw
so that the cut is up.

You can now fit the tail fins together, like this:

Now throw the straw with the tail fins
across the room. It flies through the air
in a straight line!

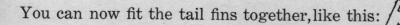
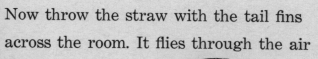
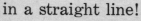

13

The Indians knew

that it is easier to pull things
than to carry them.

They took two long, strong branches
and made a "drag." This was also called
a "travois" (tra-vwah'). Some Indians
moved often from place to place. These Indians
used the travois to drag the things they took
with them when they moved.

14

Today

we can use a cart to bring home food
from the grocery store.
The cart is a drag, too.
But it has wheels.

You

can prove that it is easier to pull things
than to carry them.
Do this:
Carry a heavy bundle of books across the room.
Now put the books on a chair.
Tip the chair and pull it across the room.

Do you agree that it is easier to pull things
than to carry them?

15

The Indians knew

how to keep some foods from spoiling
by drying them.

They dried meat and fish by hanging them
in the sunshine. They also dried these foods
over their fires. Then the meat and fish
could keep for a long time without spoiling.

Today

we dry some fruits and vegetables

so that they will not spoil.

We dry grapes in the hot sun to get raisins.

We dry plums to get prunes.

You

can prove that when foods have been dried,

they do not spoil.

Put some grapes and a plum

and some raisins and prunes in a dish.

Leave them on the table.

After a few days, look at the food in the dish.

The grapes and the plum will be spoiled.

But the dried fruits — the raisins and prunes

— will still be good to eat.

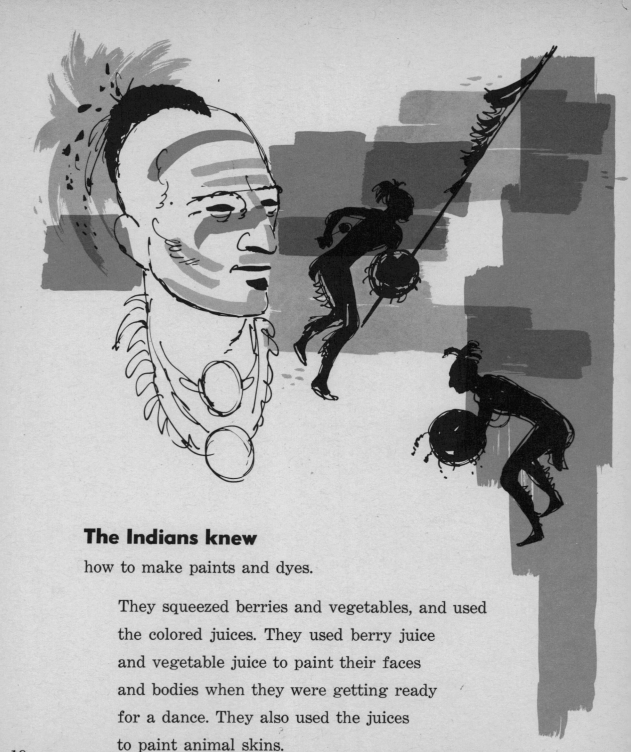

The Indians knew

how to make paints and dyes.

They squeezed berries and vegetables, and used
the colored juices. They used berry juice
and vegetable juice to paint their faces
and bodies when they were getting ready
for a dance. They also used the juices
to paint animal skins.

18

Today

we use vegetable coloring to paint toys.

You

can make your own dyes.
You need some berries and a beet.

Squeeze some berries — raspberries or
strawberries or blackberries — into a dish.

Put a sliced beet in a little water
in another dish.

Dip a small piece of white cloth
into the juice of the berries. The cloth
will have the color of the berries
dyed right into it.

Now dip another piece of white cloth
into the juice of the beet.
This cloth will have the color of the beet
dyed into it.

The Indians knew

that sound goes through the ground.

When they wanted to hear sounds from far off,
they put their ears to the ground
and listened.

Today

we knock on the door before we go into
a room. The sound goes through the solid door.
Then it goes through the air to the ears
of the people inside the room.

You

can prove that sound goes through solid things.

Rest your head on the end of your table.
Stretch your arm and scratch the other end
of the table with your fingernails.
You can hear the sound of the scratching
through the table top. You will be surprised
how loud that little scratch will sound.

The Indians knew

that rubbing makes things hot.

Sometimes rubbing can start a fire.
The Indians did not know about matches.
They rubbed two pieces of dry wood together.
They rubbed the wood until they got
some fine wood dust.
Then they rubbed until the wood dust
became so hot it began to burn.
With this burning wood dust the Indians
started their fire.

Today

Boy Scouts sometimes start a campfire
the same way the Indians did.

You

can prove that rubbing makes things hot.

Rub the palms of your hands together
very fast and very hard.
Do you feel the heat?

The Indians knew

how to make plants grow better.

Some Indians used fish to feed the plants.
When they planted corn or beans or pumpkins,
they put fish in the ground.
The fish made the plants grow better.

Today

farmers put special plant foods in the ground.

These plant foods are called fertilizers.

Some fertilizers are made from fish.

The fertilizers make the plants grow better.

You

can prove that plant food makes plants grow better.

You will need:

a dish of water, 2 dishes of sand,

6 dried lima beans, and some plant food.

(You can get plant food at the 10-cent store.)

Put all the beans in the dish of water.

The next day, take them out.

Plant 3 beans in one dish of sand.

Put the plant food in the dish.

Plant 3 beans in the other dish of sand.

Do NOT put plant food in this dish.

Water the plants every day for 7 or 8 days.

Then you will see which dish will have better plants.

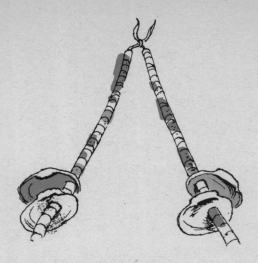

The Indians knew

that rubbing makes things wear away.

They rubbed pointed stones against shells.
They did this to make holes
through the shells.
Then they used the shells to make
strings of beads.

Today

the dentist uses a drill to rub away
the decayed parts of the teeth.

We drill rocks in the earth to get oil
and to get well water. The drilling wears
a hole through the rocks.
Then if there is oil or water,
we can bring it up through the hole.

You

can prove that rubbing makes things wear away.
Rub a nail file against your fingernails.
Watch the ends of your fingernails wear away.

The Indians knew

that many things float in water.

> They knew that logs can float for many miles.
> They cut down trees. Then they tied
> some tree trunks together to make a raft.
> They went floating down the river
> on these rafts.

Today

lumbermen cut down trees.

They put the logs into the river.

The logs float down the river to a mill.

There they are cut up into boards.

You

can prove that some things float

when they are put into water.

Drop a nail, a piece of wood, a small stone,

and a coin into a pan of water.

Which things sink?

Which things float?

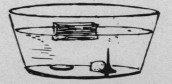

The Indians knew

how to use the moon as a calendar.
They knew that there is a full moon
about every 29 days.

Today

the number of days in the month on our calendar
is almost the same as the number of days
in the "moon month" of the Indians.

You

too can use the moon as a calendar.

Watch the sky every night if you can.
The first time you see a full moon,
make a dot on a piece of paper.

Make a dot every night until there is
another full moon. Then count the dots.

How many do you have? That is how many days
there are in a "moon month." Now look
at your calendar and count the number of days
in the month. Do a "moon month" and a calendar
month have almost the same number of days?

Now you know some of the things
the Indians knew.

The Indians knew how to use what they found
around them.

They knew how to do many things
that we still do today.